My Huey – Loss of a Dear Little Pomeranian

By Victoria Nelson-Flores

© 2011 by Victoria Nelson-Flores. All rights reserved.
Published by Lulu.com

ISBN 978-1-257-18727-0

"The dog is the most faithful of animals and would be much esteemed were it not so common. Our Lord God has made His greatest gifts the commonest."

-- Martin Luther

Dedicated to my Huey, who brought me and my husband so much joy and happiness for such a small creature. I'll never forget you. And also dedicated to all the Poms we've had in the past and the ones we'll have in the future. There will always be Poms in my life – I just can't live without them.

Vicki Nelson-Flores
March 2011

My Huey

I began writing this story less than a week after March 4, 2011 - the day I had to make the most heart wrenching decision of my life - to put my dear little Pomeranian, Huey, to sleep. He would have been fourteen years old in two months and with us for nearly eleven years. He had been ill for two days and we didn't know what exactly was going on. He'd thrown up the last meal he had and wouldn't eat or drink water. He had one incident of what can only be described as projectile diarrhea. He would have moments of rest and then other moments where it seemed he couldn't get comfortable - he would change position over and over again. A vet visit only told us his white blood count was a bit high and one of his kidney functions was a bit high - nothing earth shattering. Huey was also a little dehydrated. Not surprising as he wasn't drinking and had been throwing up and had diarrhea. The doctor thought perhaps a bacteria of some kind had gotten into his system and was messing with Huey's digestive process. When he did a fecal exam on Huey there was evidence of blood which also helped me confirm that his earlier diarrhea was also blood although I didn't know it at the time. He gave me a liquid antibiotic to give Huey every twelve hours. He also suggested the possibility of taking Huey to the emergency veterinarian hospital in nearby Annapolis so that IV fluids could be administered to help with the dehydration. I asked the doctor if I could take him home and give him water every hour with his medicine dropper to keep him hydrated – I wanted to try to help him myself rather than just leave him in a strange place. The vet agreed, so that's what I did. That was Wednesday. I took him home and gave him his first dose of antibiotic. He had no interest in food. Sometimes he'd walk to his water bowl but then he'd stand there. I guess he was still feeling some nausea. I would give him water with his medicine dropper every hour….sometimes it stayed down, sometimes it didn't. There was no change by that night in Huey even though I was getting water into him. Often it seemed he'd throw it up too soon for any of it to be absorbed by his little six pound body. I worried about him and said many prayers, hoping that whatever was bothering him would soon pass. Wednesday night he seemed to be able to sleep more than the night before and my hopes were raised that maybe he was starting to feel just a little bit better.

  Thursday came and he was back to sometimes resting comfortably and other times he was very restless. I called the vet again to ask a couple questions and get his opinion. I decided to keep trying to help Huey at home, still thinking it was some kind of intestinal bug. He would cry out a little every once in a while and I thought that it was because he was having some kind of stomach cramping. I'd pick him up and sooth him and talk to him – trying in every way I could think of to help him. Thursday night he had a difficult time relaxing – neither he nor I got much sleep. Late that night he started throwing up a dark substance – at the time I didn't think it was blood. It wasn't red or black looking. I figured it was some sort of bile from his little stomach being empty for so long. He seemed weak and at times limp, and I really feared he wouldn't make it through the night. I talked to him a lot that night and prayed over him. The next morning I made the decision to take him to the emergency vet hospital in Annapolis. He got into his little carrier on his own and then just laid there for the twenty minute trip. I left our other Pom, Hershey, at home.

    When I got to the vet hospital they took him from me immediately to begin work on him. The doctor talked with me and took down information. I told her all the details about Huey's illness over the last couple of days. I took the towel out of his carrier and started wiping my hands all over it – on both sides. I wanted to put it in his cage so he'd have something that smelled familiar to him. The first thing they did when they took him from me was take blood from him. I waited in the exam room for the results and when they came back it wasn't good. His kidney levels were so high they were immeasurable. They were failing. His temperature was ten degrees lower than normal. It seemed my Huey was dying. I could not believe it. I cried and cried thinking that I probably wouldn't be taking him home alive. The doctor explained different tests and treatments that they would do but since Huey also had a heart murmur, they had to be careful. Some of the very things you can do to help the kidneys can be hard on the heart. They would do all they could and we would just have to see what would happen. Huey definitely wasn't coming home with me that day – perhaps he'd have to be hospitalized for a few days. The doctor left the room and came back with some paperwork. One sheet listed the various tests and treatment planned for him. It also listed the low end of the cost for everything and the high end. At that point I didn't care about cost – I was going to pay

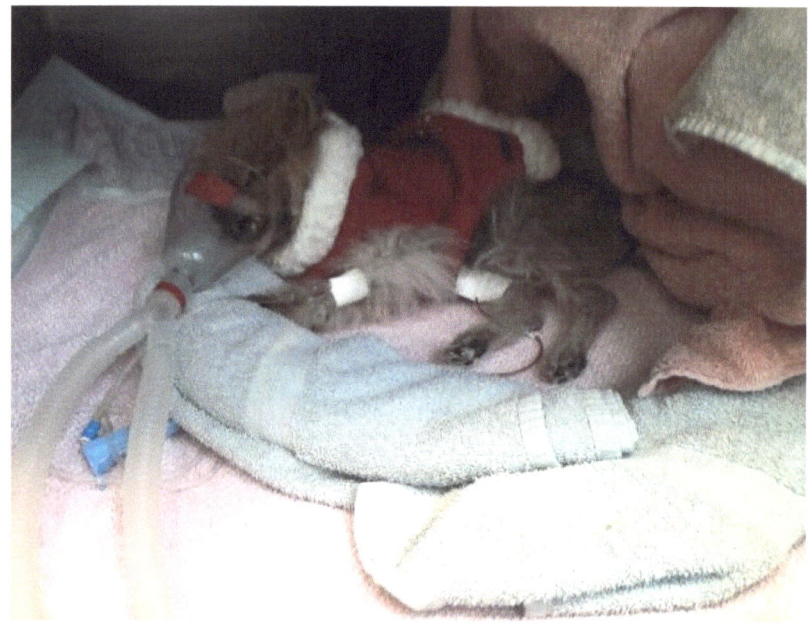

whatever it took to give Huey a chance. The doctor and I talked some more and she said I could go back and see Huey. They took me back to see him in the little pet intensive care unit. There he was, this little tiny dog, in a cage surrounded by soft towels. He only weighed 5.1 pounds at this point – just two days before he was 5.8 pounds. I placed the towel that I had wiped my hands all over in with him – putting it near his face so he could smell it. They had rolled up one towel to make a little raised area where he could rest his head. There was also a warming pad under the towels to help bring up his temperature. The IV was in his front leg. He was lying down and when I began petting him he stood up and I put my hands on each side of him to steady him. I think he stood up because he wanted me to pick him up – he always did that at home when I came over to him. I helped him to lie back down and continued petting and talking to him. I leaned into his cage and kissed his little head and cheek. My heart was breaking. I felt like I was in a dream, like this wasn't really happening.

The doctor showed me his x-rays – his heart was enlarged. She explained a lot to me but I have to admit I don't remember everything – as I listened to her I was only focused on hearing something positive. Unfortunately she didn't have much in the way of positive information for me. I went back over to Huey's cage and after spending about forty-five minutes or so with him I left to go home. My husband and I planned to go back to see Huey when he got home from work later that afternoon.

It's so ironic – two of the heart medications Huey was on for the last four years can be hard on the kidneys and we all knew that when he started taking them. That's why we had his blood tested once a year. But he needed them – he'd been having little collapsing episodes because of his heart murmur and the medications gave him over four more years with no collapsing. So the very medicines that helped prolong his life ended up being a major factor in taking it.

When I got home I went upstairs and lay on the bed with little Hershey – numb with fear and sadness and grief. I pulled Huey's little bed over to me so I could rest my hand in it. I picked up the little plush pillow toy from the bed and smelled it – it smelled like Huey. The TV was on to make sound but I wasn't really paying attention to it. Hershey slept near me, having no idea of the agony I was going through.

After a couple hours I called the hospital to see how Huey was – the doctor was with an emergency case but the lady who answered went back to look at Huey and he was the same as when I had been there. She said she'd have the doctor call me. Within about thirty minutes I got the call. I still have the number in our caller ID…..she called at 2:45. She told me that earlier when they tried to put a catheter into Huey to measure urine output he became very distressed and his breathing became so labored that they stopped to let him relax. But his breathing never went back to normal. He had also thrown up some blood. Then she asked me a question that made my heart sink – did I want them to resuscitate Huey if he went into cardiac arrest. The same type of question the doctors asked me about my dad in 2005. A terrible question to have to answer. I told her that based on what she was telling me I thought it best not to stress his little body anymore by trying to revive him. I prayed I was making the right decision. Things were not looking good at all. She said she knew my husband and I were planning to come see Huey later that afternoon but she thought I should come now. Huey was in danger of going into cardiac arrest. So off I went, fearing I might not get there in time.

Huey was still alive when I got there. He did have the catheter now – a second attempt had been successful. He was lying there with an IV tube in his front leg, the catheter to measure urine, and a small trumpet shaped tube near his nose giving him oxygen to help him. He was panting a little. He knew I was there. Again, I talked to him and petted him, kissed his little head, trying to reassure and soothe him. But inside, my world was crashing down. This little guy who had been in my life for nearly eleven years was in danger of leaving my world at any moment. The doctor let me be with him but she stopped by several times to talk with me. Huey's situation was not going to get better. I believed that now. The catheter was not showing any urine production at all even after being on IV fluids for several hours......his kidneys were not functioning.

Huey's cardiologist works in the same facility and when he found out Huey had been admitted, he came over and hugged me. I lost it – this is the same doctor who just about four years earlier had called Huey the little miracle dog. After being diagnosed with a heart murmur and being on medications for three months we had gone back for a follow up echocardiogram. The test results were so good that the cardiologist was amazed. An answer to my prayers for sure.

One of the papers I had signed was a euthanasia form just in case it came to that. I chose the option of taking Huey's body for a home burial......just seeing those words and knowing they were referring to my Huey tore me up inside.

I called my husband and told him that Huey was not looking good and there was a real possibility we'd have to make the decision to let him go. He said that whatever decision I made was alright with him. We hung up and I continued to pet Huey and talk to him. He knew I was there – he would look at me and his ears would perk up once in a while when he heard one of the other nearby dogs let out a bark. But he was distressed. He wasn't getting better. While standing there spending my last moments with my little one, I suddenly remembered that my new cell phone I'd gotten less than two weeks earlier has a camera in it. So I got it out and took two photos of Huey lying in his little hospital cage.

Once more his doctor stopped by to see how both Huey and I were doing. I nodded to her that it was time – I couldn't let him be in so much discomfort any longer. And there was no hope of reversing his condition. I had my final moments with Huey – kissed his little head one last time. She came back a few minutes later with two syringes. So, at 4:15 a sedative was injected into his IV line….in just a couple seconds his little body was relaxed…..the panting stopped. Then she quickly administered the fatal dose into the IV line with the second syringe and it was over. She took her stethoscope and listened for his heartbeat – there was none. My Huey was gone. I couldn't believe what I was seeing. It was so surreal – like I wasn't really there to witness this. So many thoughts raced through my mind.

Just three days ago he was his usual little self – going crazy for lunch and treats......being happy and affectionate with us. Enjoying his life. And now this. And so quickly.

One of the ladies offered to get Huey's carrier out of my car and she brought it back in. The doctor wrapped little Huey in the towel that had been in his carrier and gently placed him in it. The same towel I had wiped my hands all over earlier. I asked if there was a back door we could use – she said yes. She carried Huey for me and we went to my car. She hugged me as we said good bye and said how sorry she was. I got in the car and just sat there in disbelief. This wasn't supposed to happen like this. It was just supposed to be an upset digestive tract – not a life threatening condition. Not a terminal condition. Just three days ago he was fine and now he's gone? How am I supposed to process this huge loss in my mind?

I called my husband while still sitting in the car to tell him that Huey was gone. I also called Shari, the lady we bought Huey from. She and I both cried on the phone when I told her the news. She knew how much Huey meant to me. Then I began the drive home. Most of the time I drove with one hand because I had the other hand resting on Huey's body. He was still warm and I wanted to feel that warmth for as long as I could.

When I got home I immediately began preparing Huey's little burial container. I'd bought it several years earlier to have on hand, dreading the day I'd use it. I gathered up all his little shirts and sweaters and folded each one neatly and placed them in the bottom of the container. Huey had quite a wardrobe as he'd had fur loss issues for several years. No medical reason was ever found for it and since Poms can often have these fur loss issues we just learned to live with it. It caused him no discomfort. On top of the clothing I placed the towel Huey was wrapped in and then I laid Huey on the towel and brought one edge of the towel up near his neck. I set the little container on the floor and tilted it a little so Hershey could see. I wanted him to understand that Huey was gone now. He came over and sniffed a little, not getting too close and backed away.

    I waited for my husband to get home. I looked at Huey and stroked his little face and ears – his tiny little face. I hated the thought of not seeing that little face look up at me ever again…..not seeing that little face between his two front paws while he slept. How I would miss that little baby face and those big round eyes.

    When my husband arrived we both stood and looked down at little Huey. So hard to believe. He was such a huge part of our everyday lives. We put one of his favorite little crunchy treats in near his head, pulled the other end of the towel over his face and then put the lid on the container, sealing it twice with tape. It was evening now and we would bury him in the morning, out where two other little Poms are resting.

    That evening we talked, we reminisced, we looked at photo albums, still in shock. I had no trouble falling asleep but woke up while it was still dark out and couldn't get back to sleep. So many memories kept flashing through my mind…..so many thoughts and scenes about Huey. While I would miss him terribly I knew one thing – that little guy had the best life he could ever have dreamed of. And I was able to get the tiniest bit of comfort knowing that. Huey had a good life – no doubt about that.

    I had missed three days of work so I could stay home and take care of my Huey. One night I dozed off and on through the night with my hand resting on him so that if he stirred I would awaken and would be right there if he needed anything. I hated to see him uncomfortable.

    When it came time to enter my time at work for those three days I had the option of taking vacation days if I wanted to. Paid personal time is also available as is an absence without pay. I took a paid personal day for the first day and didn't feel right taking pay for the next two days as well. And I couldn't bring myself to put down vacation for days which I spent agonizing over my little one and ultimately losing him. Vacation is supposed to be a pleasant time, a fun time and I just couldn't call those days vacation. So I took no pay for those days. Some people might call me silly or foolish but so be it. Those were not vacation days to me.

    The next morning I went out to our backyard early and began gathering stones from around our yard to line the edges of Huey's little grave. When my husband was up and about he came out and began digging. The ground was soft and aside from a couple of stubborn tree roots the job went fairly smoothly. A good friend of ours from church, Pamela, had offered to come over for the burial and when she arrived all of us went outside, me carrying little Huey's casket. I kissed the lid of his casket one last time as I went out the door. Our little Hershey was with us as well. When we got to the grave I started crying and my husband and Pamela gently lowered the little casket into the ground. The hole was filled in and the three of us began lining the edge with the stones I had collected earlier. A silk plant arrangement, brought by Pamela, was taken apart and the pieces put in the soil in the grave. And it was over. All but the little stone marker I would later purchase to put on the gravesite. In my heart I mourned uncontrollably, still feeling as if I was in a dream. In my heartache, I was able to muster a happy thought - the life we gave little Huey was more than any little dog could hope for. He was loved, protected, taken care of, prayed for, and shared with our friends and family. He got to go on vacations with us twice a year, he was a good traveler. He went to Williamsburg, Luray Caverns, Ocean City-NJ, the Cape May Ferry, and Mystic, CT to name a few. He even had his own pool float that he would just snuggle down in and just float around in. When we were on vacations he was carried around in a little pouch type carrier that I wore and he got to see everything from a great vantage point. So I was a tiny bit comforted at that moment about the life he had while with us. I had no regrets. He was very much loved during his life with us, and he showed us that he loved us too. And although we've only had Hershey about two years, he too is living that same kind of life. And I'm happy for that.

    I'll never forget Huey. In fact, I've prayed to God to let me dream about him so I can see him again. I've heard the phrase some people use, 'heart dog'. A heart dog is the dog that you have an extra special bond with – a bond you haven't had with any of your other dogs even though you loved them dearly. Huey was my heart dog. We have photos and memories but life will never be the same without our little Huey in it. He was a huge, huge part of my life and thoughts every day. There was hardly a time when I didn't go up or down the stairs in our house without Huey in one arm. He had a bad knee in one of his hind legs and I didn't want him doing stairs so he was carried an awful lot. Many of the routines in my daily life revolved around Huey, even simple routines. The first time I stood at my kitchen counter fixing just one little plate of food for Hershey was a sad one. For years I'd stood there with two little plates in front of me. The three little bottles of medicine that Huey took for his heart were kept on our nightstand. Now that space is empty – another reminder that he's no longer with me. His little toothbrush – another bit of evidence of caring for my Huey. Everywhere I look there is something that reminds me of him. When I do something around the house or look at something the thought comes to my mind that 'the last time I did this' or ' the last time I looked at this' Huey was here….Huey was alive……Huey was with me when I bought this, etc. I look at his little empty bed on the luggage rack next to our bed – brings tears to my eyes. He was always in that little bed – he could see everything from there – the bathroom, the entrance to the bedroom. It was a perfect vantage point for him. It's a little cave type of bed with a roof over it and he loved it. He's the last thing I think of before I fall asleep and the first thing I think of when I wake up. I know that will pass in time but right now the reminders of his life with us are everywhere I turn and I seem to walk around each day with a huge lump in my throat. Our house feels a bit empty even with the two of us and Hershey in it. I'll be forever grateful to God for bringing Huey into our lives and despite how devastating it was to lose him I wouldn't trade the years we had with him for anything. He brought us joy, laughter, companionship and love.

Huey came into our lives in the year 2000, a couple of months after my first Pomeranian, Timber,

passed away, leaving us with one Pom, Trevor, pictured at left. Trevor was about ten years old at this time and in excellent health. My husband and I talked about whether or not to get another Pom and finally decided to start searching. I had been contacting shelters and rescue groups, anyone I could find, to see if we could find a little one that needed a good home. I wasn't having much luck at first. Then a lady, Shari, who was involved with Pomeranian Rescue emailed me back and said she had a little male that she used to show but he had gotten a little too big for the show ring and she hadn't been able to part with him as yet. He was almost three years old. She invited me to come to her house to meet the little guy and of course I was very excited to come out and see all her little Poms. The picture below shows Huey winning a dog show that was held on the Eastern Shore. I believe he was under a year old when he won this show. We corresponded via email and then talked on the phone and

made arrangements for me to come see her and the little one. She only lives about a half hour from our home and was a show breeder of Poms. I couldn't wait to get to her house to see all the little ones.

When I arrived she led me downstairs where she kept all her Poms....all sixteen or so of them. They had their own large room lined with beds and cages......little pens here and there. There was a refrigerator, sink, cabinetry and a washer/dryer. We got past the little gate to that room and I was immediately surrounded by all these adorable little furry faces all looking up at me and jumping against my legs.....all wanting my attention. I'd never seen so much cuteness in one place before.

Huey was pointed out to me and he was just a ball of fur. We managed to round him up and the three of us went into the family room part of the basement to spend some time away from the other dogs. Huey was just so lively....running back and forth across the sofa and pillows. So cute. We visited for a while and I held Huey now and then and looked into his little face. I was pretty sure he was the dog for us.

We made arrangements for Huey and Shari to visit our home so she could see the kind of environment Huey would be living in. She wasn't going to let her little one go to just anyone. She was able to meet my dad and our other Pom, Trevor. And after the visit in our home we decided to purchase him with the agreement that we would have him neutered once we were certain he would work out for us, which he did. About two months after he came to live with us we had that done. Broke my heart to leave him at the vet though that day. I can

still remember standing at the counter and the girl carrying him to the back. He looked back over her shoulder at me as if to say, 'Hey Mom, where are they taking me and why aren't you coming too?' Of course I started crying at that point – but the ladies in the office were used to emotional owners. Huey did fine and I picked him up later that day. Anyway, back to making Huey a part of our family - I signed the paperwork with Shari to make Huey a permanent part of our home and wrote the check and he was ours.

    I brought him home on St Patrick's Day in 2000, it was a Friday and I picked him up on the way home from work. I took a week of vacation time to be with him and help him get used to his two new homes (ours and my dad's). He was such a happy little dog and had a great personality and I loved getting to know him. He was an adorable fluff of fur that would run around like a little wind-up toy.

Huey and Trevor (pictured below) spent days at my dad's house and I would pick Huey up on the way home every day. Trevor spent weekends and one night during the week at our house. But Huey I just had to

have with me all the time and we never spent a night apart all the years we had him. Now Huey had two houses and two yards to play in and.....two households to spoil him and Trevor as his doggie companion.

Huey never was much for playing with dog toys or with other dogs. Every once in a while I could get him to be playful with me – I'd pretend to chase him and he'd take off running and then sneak back slowly and peek at me around the corner. I'd pretend to go after him again and he'd run off again. And in the early years about two or three times a year we might get him to chase a tennis ball but he'd never bring it back. He was more into sleeping and eating. And he loved to burrow into any blanket or load of laundry that was available. When I would take an armful of clothing from the dryer and put it on our bed to be folded Huey would always come over and start pawing around at it until he had just the right spot arranged. Then he would lie down and sleep.

We discovered that Huey really loved dog beds, especially the kind with a roof over them. So of course he had to have a bed like that at our house AND at my

dad's house. At our house we put Huey's bed on a luggage rack next to our bed so he could go back and forth between our bed and his. His favorite position while in his bed was to rest his head on the edge of it and have one little paw on each side of his muzzle. I can't count how many times I saw him sleep like that for a couple of hours or so at a time. He also loved to sleep on pillows whether it was bed pillows or sofa pillows.

He was very people and food oriented. He would bark the whole time his lunch was being fixed often spinning as the plate was lowered to the floor for him. And he learned what the word 'treat' meant real fast. We had to be careful in our conversations because if he even thought he heard the word treat – he would start barking and run toward the kitchen. And we had to watch him because he was always willing to try and steal a treat from our other Pomeranian....he'd wait till the other dog, Trevor or later, Hershey, wasn't looking and he'd run in quickly, grab the treat and then take it to his bed to eat. He just loved food and if we were sitting and eating something he always hung around close to us hoping to get a taste. The only thing I ever saw him refuse to eat in all his eleven years with us was pretzels. He'd take it from your hand, move it around in his mouth a little bit and then just spit it out and leave it on the floor. But to be honest we did try to make it a rule not to give him food from the table and for the most part we were good at sticking to that rule.

Huey learned many words over the years: treat, want, go, car, drink, water, etc. Sometimes I could just look at him and say the word go and he'd get all excited and run around wanting to go out the door and get in the car. The last few years we used little yogurt drops for treats and Huey had even learned the word yogurt.

That first year we had Huey we took him with us on our yearly spring vacation to Ocean City, NJ....his first vacation. We board the Ferry in Lewes, Delaware and take it across to Cape May, New Jersey. Then we drive about a half hour before we arrive in Ocean City.

He was a wonderful traveler and just enjoyed being with us no matter where we went. He got to ride the Cape May Ferry many times in his years with us. Sometimes we'd go up on one of the decks and watch the view and other times we just stayed in the car listening to music, talking, or having a quick snack. My husband would sometimes take a nap. The ferry has several decks and there are gift shops and snack bars available. It's a very nice trip across the Delaware Bay. Below is a photo of me holding Huey at the Cape May Ferry terminal. We took him everywhere; stores, to visit friends in the hospital, the nursing home to visit my dad, etc. Most of

the time he was carried in the little pouch type carrier that I wore. He loved it – he was close to me and he could see everything and everyone. And of course people could see him better too which meant we were often stopped by people wanting to see him or pet him. His little face was very irresistible.

The first time we walked down to the edge of the ocean waves with Huey he started shaking. Guess he'd never seen or heard anything like that before. But before long he was used to it and stopped shaking. He also went with us each November for our wedding anniversary vacation. I guess because he used to be a show dog that riding around in a car was no big deal to him - he was already used to it. He never got car sick or whined - just sat there or laid there taking a nap. As long as we were nearby he was content. At right is a photo of my husband holding Huey at one of the  Cape May Ferry terminals. When we travel we'd make the regular stops along the road so he could relieve himself and he was more than happy to hop back into his bed and continue the journey. But if we stopped to eat then he definitely had to be involved in that.

The picture below shows us with Huey, pedaling a surrey on the boardwalk at Ocean City, NJ. As we went

along we'd stop at whatever little shop interested us and then continue down the boardwalk.

We traveled with his little treats and dog food and of course a thermos of cool water for him. The dogs always had their own little overnight bag that I packed whenever we went away. Their brush, toothbrush & toothpaste, any medicines that either of them might be taking at that time, Huey's little shirts, their water bowl, a blanket for them to lay on, etc. And of course his little dog bed always came along with us – he loved being in that either in the car or at our destination. Huey always knew it was packed for him – we caught him many times sniffing around in the bag. All the comforts of home for our little guys.

Doggie birthdays at our house are always celebrated with Frosty Paws dog ice cream or plain vanilla ice cream and little pieces of a cake or Twinkie.

They love it. Huey would twirl around as his plate was being put down and by the time he was done the plate was so clean you'd never know it had been used. We never bought birthday gifts because they got everything they needed or wanted throughout the year but we never miss doing the cake and ice cream to celebrate another year of their little lives. They loved getting this special treat and danced around at my feet till I put the plates down.

After a few years I noticed Huey holding up one of his hind legs and I took him to the vet to get checked out. One of his kneecaps had slipped out of place, a fairly common problem with Poms called luxating patella and he'd need surgery. Of course I was a nervous wreck.....operate? On my Huey? But it needed to be done. I dropped him off at the vet in the morning on the day of his surgery and was able to pick him up around seven that night. He was groggy from the anesthetic and had been shaved. He had a pain medicine patch on his hip and was pretty pathetic that first night but the next morning he was a lot more alert and wanting to move a bit. I scheduled his surgery during my company's Christmas shutdown so I could be with him. His recovery was very good and he was running around in no time holding the affected leg up a bit and was soon using it normally.

    Huey went on all our vacations over the years – he never missed one.....his little bed situated in the middle in the back of whatever vehicle we were taking. He had

a great vantage point and could see everything. I loved just having him with me. We planned our trips to places where we could get a room with a kitchen in it (or a house) so we could eat in. We never left Huey alone when on vacation and it worked out quite well. And often, whether packing to leave or to come home, if a suitcase presented itself Huey would hop in and make himself at home. We have several photos take over the years of him sitting in one of our suitcases, sometimes he'd get in before we even

had any clothing in them.

There were many times over the years as we were walking that people would stop us and want to take a picture of him. When sitting in the carrier pouch all you would see was his little face and two little paws hanging over the edge. Sometimes people thought he was a little stuffed animal and would ask me if he was real. He'd sit so still while being carried around.

On one of our trips to Ocean City in New Jersey

we were walking along the boardwalk on a very sunny day. The temperatures were cool but the sun was pretty warm and I mentioned out loud that I wished I had some kind of a visor or something to shade Huey's head and face. Well, next thing I knew my husband had popped into one of the little shops there on the boardwalk and had purchased this baby bonnet type thing to put on Huey to help keep the sun off his face. He did look cute but I spent the rest of the afternoon telling people it wasn't my idea. I'm sure there were people who thought we were nuts. By the way, we saw the signs that said no dogs were allowed on the boardwalk but since Huey was carried his little feet never touched it. No laws broken, right? Makes sense to me.

  When we moved to a house with an in ground pool in 2003 there were new things to do with Huey. I

decided to get him a pool float of his very own so he could enjoy the water with us. After searching online I discovered they don't really make pool floats for dogs so I had to improvise. I bought a baby float with a little canopy over it for shade. I covered the two leg

openings with a rectangular plastic container to keep water out, put a folded beach towel on top of the container and then set Huey on the towel. Voila! He loved it. He would just make himself comfy and take a nap while floating around the pool. If it was hot out I'd take him out every so often and

let him swim a few strokes to get cooled off and put him back in the float. Over the years he had several different floats – all with a roof to keep the sun off of him. Trevor, and later Hershey, also enjoyed the pool but not in quite the same way as Huey. He just loved to sleep and the motion of the water just lulled him off. Many hours each summer were spent in the pool with Huey either in one of his floats or sleeping on the nearby canopy swing while we swam. Like always, he was content just to be near us.

    The new house also added a new challenge – it had steps going to the ground from our back deck and little Huey really didn't like stairs. Plus he'd had one leg operated on in the past and I didn't want him to use the stairs either. And our Trevor was older now too so a

ramp was a great solution to them having to go up and down steps. So I searched the internet looking for some kind of a ramp and I was able to find one. Huey had no problem getting used to it – used it immediately. Later I added a second ramp to the bottom of the first one so that the angle wasn't so steep. It was perfect. Made things so much easier for Huey and Trevor. In the winter though, when we had ice or snow I had to make sure it was cleared. It had some kind of an outdoor carpeted surface but if we had a bad ice storm the carpet could be completely covered and the dogs wouldn't be able to get any traction for walking. The last winter of Huey's life we had such an ice storm. I let the dogs (Huey and Hershey – Trevor had passed away in 2006) out and Hershey being younger, just bounded down the steps to the ground with no trouble, even though they were a bit icy. Little Huey walked over to the ramp, not knowing it was so icy, stepped onto it and promptly slid all the way down to the bottom, standing on all four feet all the way. I don't know how he was able to keep his balance but he did. It was comical to see but I was so thankful he didn't fall. I immediately started filling a bucket with hot water to take out and pour on the ramp and also across the deck to melt the ice. Had to make several trips back and forth before I had enough of the ice melted away. Poor little Huey stood at the bottom of the ramp looking up at me wanting me to help – I told him I was working as fast as I could to get him back up onto the deck. What an ordeal....I finally got enough ice melted that it was safe for both he and I to walk on and we hustled back into the house. Hershey, of course, had no problem with any of this and wondered what all the fuss was about. We also placed a small ramp in our family room leading up to one of the stuffed chairs. That way Huey could sleep on the chair or the ottoman while we were at work.

I had always used little dog treats as a reward when our dogs would go out and do what they were supposed to. Consequently they got into the habit of whenever they came back inside or if they came downstairs or if someone came home, they thought they were supposed to get a treat. If we had a visitor to our home, that visitor was required to walk to the refrigerator and get a treat for each of them. And until that happened the dogs would not relax nor would

they be quiet about it. They were entitled to a treat and by golly they were going to get it, no matter how much reminding they had to do. And if the dogs and I were downstairs and my husband arrived back home from wherever he'd been, both dogs would go scampering across the kitchen floor demanding a treat. Once they had it then they were ready for attention and holding but the treat always had to come first.

In our bedroom I keep a little water bowl on the night stand for the dogs. Several years back when we discovered the Propel flavored waters, Huey discovered he loved Propel too. If I came into the bedroom with a

Propel bottle he knew it. I'd offer him his water bowl, he'd sniff it and then turn his head, refusing to drink. But as soon as I poured in some of the Propel water he was eager to drink. His favorite flavor was grape. We started referring to him as the little water snob because so often he'd turn his nose up at his water bowl until I poured Propel into it.

    One year we decided to get a pet stroller. Thought it'd be handy for the dogs now and then. Huey was a little older now and if we went to the park or some other similar location, or if he just got tired of walking we could push him in the stroller. He'd be safe and shaded from the sun. The day the stroller arrived we assembled it and took turns pushing the dogs around the house to see how they liked it. A few days later the

stroller was still in the house and I couldn't find Huey anywhere. Looked all over for him. Then I spied him. He had discovered the little carry all area on the bottom of the stroller, climbed in and was sleeping away.

And that wasn't the first time this happened. Whenever the stroller was in the house you could bet that Huey would find it and make himself at home in the bottom of it. I don't think many people were used to seeing a dog being pushed in a stroller so we tended to attract attention when using it. But once they saw little Huey they were all smiles and wanting to pet him and know what his name was, etc. Huey seemed to love being pushed around in his stroller and he could stretch out and lie down if he wanted to.

Huey loved to sleep. Even when he was very young he would sleep a lot. On our bed he'd get up on the

pillow facing away from the headboard and just nod off. On vacations to the Jersey shore, while waiting for the Cape May Ferry, we'd put a blanket up on the dashboard and set him up there. He'd lay there a while and nod off now and then. On the just over an hour long Ferry ride we'd leave him up there and he'd get a nice nap. Often when traveling home at night in the

car he'd fall asleep in my arms. He always looked so cute when he was sleeping. He must have felt so safe and secure while I was holding him.

    Brushing doggie teeth was a nightly ritual. Huey had his teeth cleaned at the vet when he was younger but I never liked the idea of having to put him under

anesthesia. Plus, once he got older and developed the heart murmur I definitely didn't want him put under unless it was absolutely necessary. So I began brushing his teeth each night before going to bed. I found toothpaste made for dogs that had a flavor to it and he really liked it. In fact, he came to like the process so much that he would come over to me each evening waiting to get his teeth brushed. Sometimes all I had to do was look over at him and he'd come to me. He was so used to this happening every night and he looked forward to it. I found it so comical – a little dog coming to you because he wants his teeth brushed. I also found a small tooth scaler to help clean any tartar off of his teeth. I did the best I could to keep him from having to be put under anesthesia. He had almost all his teeth when he passed away...most of the ones he lost were the little tiny ones in the very front of his mouth.

    Huey also attended many of our church functions. He was even the subject of a Children's Story one Sabbath just before the sermon and the little kids just loved seeing him at the end of the story. The story was about how God had answered a lady's prayer when her little dog was diagnosed with a heart murmur. He had improved so much after being on his medications.   I told the story in the third person and at the end of the story I told them the lady in the story was me and the little dog was Huey. My husband then came walking out with Huey in his arms and brought him over for the kids to see and pet. It was hard for me not to get emotional over Huey and my eyes did get teary seeing Huey carried out. I knew how worried I had been when he was first diagnosed with his heart murmur and I was so thankful that he was doing so well on his medications. I said a lot of prayers over that little guy. To watch him you'd never know he had a heart problem at all. He'd scamper around and spin in circles for his food just like he always did.   I'd always hoped I'd have many more years with him in our lives. At the end of the story I gave each of the children a little plush dog to keep to help them remember the story and remind them that God does hear our prayers. I had been a bit nervous about bringing Huey for the story but everything went very well and I was glad I'd brought him in.

Later, Hershey (shown sitting on the back of our chair in the picture below) too, was the subject of a Children's Story and at the end of the story my husband came out carrying both Huey and Hershey. They were so

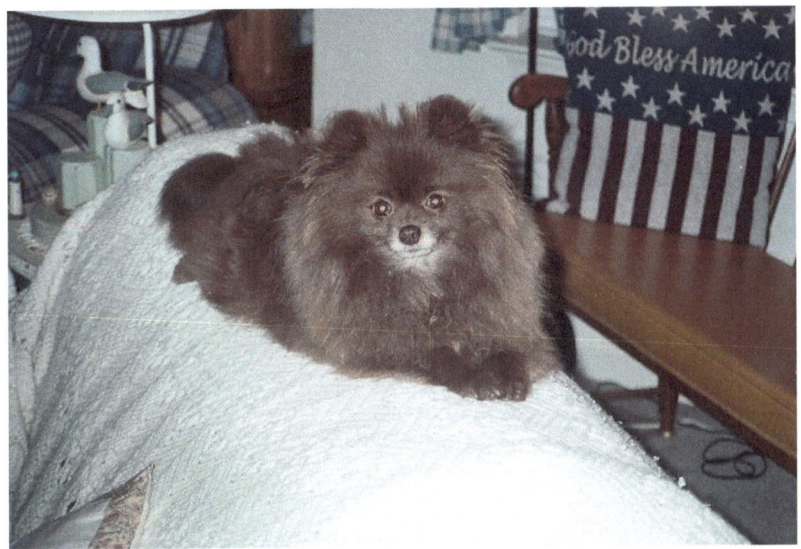

good in the church and when the story was over I took them back to the mother's room for the remainder of the service. I was so happy that I could share them with our church and people always seemed to look forward to seeing them. Our Poms also attended church picnics and Saturday night socials from time to time. They've even been known to attend a vespers service now and then, sitting quietly with me in the back.

One evening we were putting groceries away at home. Some of the items had to go into the pantry which had two doors. Suddenly I noticed Huey wasn't around....my husband and I looked all over – couldn't find him anywhere. Then I opened one of the pantry doors and there was Huey just standing there in the dark.

He'd gone in apparently to sniff around when the door was open and we hadn't noticed it. We guessed he was probably in there for about five minutes. He never made a sound – just stood there waiting for someone to let him out. He was never a whiny type dog and I guess he figured that sooner or later we'd open the door and let him out.

Several years back I found a pop-up Christmas dog house in some catalog I received at home. It looked adorable and immediately I thought of Huey. He loved

having something over him and I figured he would love this at Christmas time. I ordered it and when it came it literally popped up – so easy to put together. It came with a roof that attached with Velcro and it had little icicles hanging from it. Also had a chimney that attached to the roof – just the cutest thing. It also came with a pad inside and we added a towel so Huey could make a nest if he wanted to. Later we put in a little bed of faux sheepskin. This now became one of our Christmas traditions – when we would be getting out all

our Christmas decorations we would also get out the Huey Christmas House. He loved it and looked adorable in it. None of our other Poms had ever shown any interest in the little house so I wonder now if we'll ever be able to use it again. I'll keep it for now and I hope one day to see a little Pom sleeping in it again. Since Huey had fur loss, Christmas was also a time that I could put cute little Christmassy sweaters and shirts on him. He never seemed to mind and I was glad he had them to help keep him warm. And he looked so adorable in them. My all time favorite winter sweater was a little red one with the white fur trim – the same one we buried him in. Another cute little Christmas shirt had the words Santa's Little Helper on it. We had a little stocking that we hung on the fireplace screen each year. Many years we'd put some of Huey's treats in it and watch him try to get them out.

If there was snow outside Huey would always

love to stop and eat it. Even when the temperature outside was way below freezing. I always worried he'd give himself a little doggie brain freeze by eating snow in such cold weather so I'd stop him after he ate a couple of mouthfuls....but he did enjoy it. Never played in it, just wanted to eat it.

He had many, many endearing ways that presented themselves the longer we had him. When I would talk to him he'd tilt his little head back and forth as I spoke to him – it was adorable to watch – just made me want to talk more to him just to watch his head tilting. And if anyone ever picked him up, even my husband, Huey would keep his eyes on me the whole time – as if he didn't want me to be out of his sight.

Sometimes we'd give the dogs little rawhide chews which they seemed to love. Huey would get real possessive of his – so possessive that if you tried to pick him up he'd make the funniest snarling sound – your hand didn't have to be anywhere near his rawhide but he was going to complain about it just the same. This cute little dog trying to be so ferocious about his toy. You couldn't help but laugh at him.

In the last few years of his life he started doing what I can only call a kind of a head butt when he was

happy, greeting you upon coming home or just wanting to be affectionate. You had to be sitting for this – he'd come over to you rather quickly with his head down and head butt you, rubbing his little head against your arm or leg. If you scratched his back while he would do this, he'd swing his hips back and forth like he was doing a little dance. He looked adorable doing it and I regret that we never caught that on video. If he wanted attention he'd come over and nuzzle your hand or arm and look up at you. I never failed to melt at seeing that

little face. If I was sitting in a chair or on the sofa he'd come over to be picked up. But he always turned around so he was facing away from me so I could just put my hand under him and lift him. It was so cute......he was doing what he could to make it easier to be picked up. Often when I would hold him in one arm he would lay his little head down on my chest, just under my chin, content to be close. It almost brought tears to my eyes when he did that because it was such an obvious sign that he loved me and enjoyed being close.

    In the last few years I started calling him the little kiss dispenser. I'd hold him up and as soon as my face got anywhere close to his he'd give me a quick little kiss on the nose. I'd back away and come toward him again, another little kiss. It was so cute. He was so photogenic and over the years we took many photos of him - our albums have little Huey photos scattered all through them. There are pictures of him on my desk at work and on my home and work computers. There are pictures of all of my Poms in a little album that I carry in my purse. He'll always be with me.

When my dad passed away in 2005 I just had to include our Huey and Trevor. They were as much a part of dad's family as I was. I asked the funeral home director if they could come to the viewing and service which were both on the same day and he said it was fine as long as they were restrained. I was so happy - they were there, in the dog stroller. Dad would have wanted them there and I was comforted a little by their presence. He watched over them every day at his house for years while we were at work and they were great company for him. I took them to the cemetery too for the short service….they were our family and I was so pleased they were allowed to be present.

I know that God didn't answer my prayers to save Huey this time but He did answer one prayer. Every morning when I left for work, leaving the two little dogs at home alone I'd pray that He'd look after them and protect them from harm and illness. And I prayed that as Huey got older and had his heart murmur that he wouldn't die alone at home. I worried so about that. And that prayer was answered. I was with Huey night and day for the last three days of his life and I'm thankful for that. I said many prayers over him, some silent and some out loud through tears.

I've always been fascinated and touched by the bond that can develop between a human being and an animal. Completely different creations and yet they can develop a close friendship. A remarkable trait that God instilled in our little pets.....and our larger ones too. They respond to kindness and affection and care and are more than willing to show us affection as well. Over the years I've often been moved to tears at how close I was with Huey. I would look at him and think how much I would miss him when the day came that I would lose him. Before I knew it, I'd be in tears. I didn't want to think about that day. If I left the room he was in he would come searching for me. Even if it meant trying to go upstairs. I'd always try to prevent that though – I didn't want him going up stairs with his leg issues and his heart murmur. I didn't want him to exert himself. But he was always determined to find me if I didn't return to the same room within a reasonable amount of time. He just wanted to be with me, no matter where I was. And I was always happiest when I was with him.....all was right in my world when I was with my Huey. Even if he was sound asleep and not interacting with me, just being there was enough to make me happy. Guess that proves the scientific reports that say spending time with and touching your pets can lower your blood pressure and is good for your well being. I personally believe it makes the pet feel calm and peaceful too. Such unconditional love – all they want is to be with you. Even in my grief, I continue to thank God for bringing little Huey into our lives.....he was such a blessing.

And I also thank God that I had a cell phone with a camera so I could take those last two pictures of our Huey at the hospital the day he died. I had gone back and forth on the decision to get a new phone for about three months. About a week and a half before Huey passed, the day I got my new phone, I took two pictures of Huey at home in his little red sweater to try out the new feature. They were the last pictures of him before he got sick. I had no idea then how important those two pictures would later become to me. It was so easy to get him to pose – just talk to him and his little head would start tilting this way and that. We printed some copies of this photo on photo paper and have put them in frames. One is on my desk at work and one on the nightstand in our bedroom. Just a few weeks earlier I had, for the first time, trimmed the fur shorter around his face. I thought that with his fur loss it might look better. And it did. When I was done he looked so cute....like a little puppy. Those last two photos are the  only ones of him with his face trimmed. This one is my favorite. We just loved his new look! I was holding him on my lap with one hand and took the picture holding the camera in the other. Another thing I'm thankful to God for - that I was able to get this last photo of him. Who could resist that little face?

As a Christian, I've often talked with people about whether or not our pets will be in heaven with us. Some people say they have enough to worry about just making sure they themselves make it, let alone their pets. Some people are sure they'll see their pets in heaven. Others just aren't sure. But when someone has a special bond with their pets, it is something we think about. Just as we hope we'll see family members and friends again, we also hope that God, in His mercy and love for us, will allow us to be reunited with our dear pets. There is no Biblical evidence to say they will or won't be. We know God cares about the animals - He saved them in the ark when He sent a flood to the earth. So perhaps, in His love and care for us, He'll recreate our pets to live with us in heaven. We just don't know for sure. But I pray to God that He will allow our pets to be with us. They are so much a part of our lives here on earth and give us so much joy. I like to hope that I'll see Huey again, with two good knees, no heart murmur, and a thick coat of fur - healthy and perfect, just as God intended, as well as all the other pets I've had over the years. I thank God for each of them.

www.ingramcontent.com/pod-product-compliance
Lightning Source LLC
Chambersburg PA
CBHW041607220426
43666CB00001B/12